W9-CST-118

THE LITTLE
SOUP
COOKBOOK

The Little
SOUP
Cookbook

ULTIMATE
EDITIONS

First published by Ultimate Editions in 1996

© 1996 Anness Publishing Limited

Ultimate Editions is an imprint of
Anness Publishing Limited
1 Boundary Row
London SE1 8HP

This edition distributed in Canada by
Book Express, an imprint of
Raincoast Books Distribution Limited

ISBN 1 86035 188 3

Publisher Joanna Lorenz
Senior Cookery Editor Linda Fraser
Assistant Editor Emma Brown
Designer Patrick McLeavey
Illustrator Anna Koska
Photographers Michael Michaels, James Duncan, Steve Baxter,
Amanda Heywood & Michelle Garrett
Recipes Roz Denny, Catherine Atkinson, Hilaire Walden, Annie
Nichols, Norma MacMillan, Carole Clements, Elizabeth Wolf-
Cohen, Carla Capalbo, Laura Washburn, Liz Trigg, Sarah Gates,
Sue Maggs, Jenny Stacey & Alex Barker

For all recipes, quantities are given in both metric and
imperial measures, and, where appropriate, measures are
also given in standard cups and spoons. Follow one set, but not a mixture
because they are not interchangeable.

Printed in China

Contents

Introduction   6

Classic Soups   12

Fish & Meat Soups   24

Vegetable Soups   36

Chilled Summer Soups   46

Bean, Lentil & Grain Soups   54

Index   64

Introduction

Say soup and most people immediately conjure up an image of a steaming bowl served in a cosy kitchen on a cold winter's day. That's true as far as it goes, but soup can be so much more: a cool slither to soothe the throat, a sophisticated starter, a nourishing travelling companion, even a meal in itself.

The days when every household had a never-empty stock pot may have gone, but there's much to be said for reviving the art of making excellent stocks and soups, at least during the colder months. Home-made soup is delicious, nutritious, and inexpensive to make. Get into the habit of saving the water in which vegetables are cooked, set mushroom caps, celery tops and parsley stalks aside, and don't wrap that leftover roast chicken in foil and leave it to languish at the back of the fridge. Instead, pop all these ingredients into a large pan, add chopped vegetables and perhaps some soaked haricot beans and the house will soon be filled with the satisfying aroma of simmering soup. Imagine how smug you'll feel when you serve it — and have enough for tomorrow's lunch!

Soup is so gloriously agreeable. Everyday soup — the sort you make by raiding the pantry and vegetable basket — does not demand precise quantities, nor does it need to be watched over. Most hot soups benefit from long, slow cooking, and are often even better next day. Leftovers can be served precisely as before, or used as the basis of another soup which may taste entirely different. Many canned or packet soups are very good, but they do tend to betray their origins; add an appropriate can or packet to a home-made soup however, and the effect will be to intensify the flavour already there.

In recent years, soup has fallen from favour somewhat on the formal dinner menu. Warm salads, vegetable terrines and tiny tartlets have topped the popularity poll, with the average restaurant merely offering a single soup as a sop to those demanding a wider choice. Perhaps it's time to take stock of the situation. A bowl of Borscht is every bit as beautiful as a carefully crafted salad, and a chilled avocado soup will cheer even the most jaded palate. When planning a meal for meat eaters and vegetarians alike, start with Chilled Asparagus or Leek, Parsnip & Ginger Soup, follow with a simple main course served with an interesting salad, and

all your guests will be well satisfied. And for a simple – and highly successful – party, make three or four different soups, leave them simmering over a low heat, set out a selection of breads and rolls, and simply invite guests to help themselves.

Every nation has its own soups and there are few foods which more strongly evoke a sense of place. Remember spooning up Gazpacho under a Spanish moon or marvelling at the colours and flavours in a bowl of Bouillabaisse? French Onion Soup is imitated the world over, but if you've ever eaten it at midnight in Les Halles, you'll never forget the experience.

Sup your way through the soups in this collection, from classics, such as Minestrone, to the freshly innovative Melon & Basil Soup and hearty Pasta & Bean Soup – the experience is sure to bowl you over!

Types of Soup

BISQUE

Usually made from puréed shellfish, such as lobster, crab or scallops, this is a rich, creamy soup.

CHOWDER

This is the sort of soup you could make a meal of. Originally made exclusively from fish or shellfish, with bacon and vegetables (especially potatoes), it may today include other ingredients. The liquid is usually milk.

CONSOMME

A clarified soup based on meat, chicken or game stock, this owes its excellent flavour to long, slow cooking. It is always clear and may be served hot or cold and jellied.

GARBURE

A French speciality, this is a thick vegetable soup made from beans, herbs and plenty of garlic, plus a piece of preserved ham, duck, goose or turkey.

MADRILENE

A beautiful clear consommé with a deep ruby colour, thanks to the addition of tomatoes. It is often served chilled and lightly jellied.

POTAGE

This is a thick soup, based on a vegetable, poultry or fish purée.

STOCK

The liquid that forms the basis of an excellent soup, made by cooking meaty bones or fish trimmings with vegetables and flavourings. Pure vegetable stock is also widely used.

VELOUTE

This is a soup enriched with cream and/or egg yolks.

Garnishes

CROUTONS

Tiny bread cubes, fried in a mixture of oil and butter (or toasted for today's fat-conscious cooks) are very popular. Try ciabatta croûtons for a change.

ALMONDS

Toasted flaked almonds are often sprinkled on top of creamy soups just before serving.

CHEESE

Grated Parmesan cheese is essential for minestrone and similar robust soups.

BACON

Crumbled grilled bacon is delicious on a thick bean or potato soup.

CREAM

A swirl of cream looks lovely on tomato or green pea soup. Dot the cream, then swirl with a skewer.

FILO SHREDS

Fine strips of filo pastry, drizzled with oil and baked until crisp, add colour and crunch to creamy soups.

PASTA

Small pasta shapes can be used as a garnish. Add them for the final few minutes of cooking, so that they retain a bit of a bite.

HERBS

Chopped parsley or chervil is good on a clear mixed vegetable soup, while snipped chives are the classic garnish for vichyssoise, especially when served cold.

VEGETABLE SHAPES

Carrots, celeriac or swedes, cut into matchsticks or shaped with aspic cutters, look good in clear soups.

AVOCADO CUBES OR SLICES

An unusual garnish for a hot clear soup. Float on top just before serving.

Techniques

MAKING STOCK

For rich meat stock, roast shin or marrow bones with shin or neck meat in a moderately hot oven until browned *(below left)*, then add to a large saucepan containing some thickly sliced,

browned vegetables (1 onion, 1 carrot and 2 celery sticks). Pour in water to cover the mixture by twice its depth, then add some flavourings, such as peppercorns and a bouquet garni. Bring the liquid slowly to the boil. Skim any scum from the surface *(top right)* and simmer the stock, skimming the surface regularly, for about 4–5 hours. Strain the stock *(bottom left)* and degrease it before use (see facing page).

For chicken stock, cut up a meaty chicken carcass *(above left)*, chop some vegetables and place in a saucepan. Cover with water, add flavourings and simmer for 2 hours. Strain *(above right)*.

For fish stock, place fish trimmings (heads, skin and bones but not gills, which give a bitter flavour) in a saucepan. Add some chopped onion and celery, with white peppercorns, parsley and some dry white wine, if liked. Cover with water *(above left)*, bring to the boil and simmer, skimming from time to time, for a maximum of 40 minutes. Strain *(above right)*.

For vegetable stock, chop a mixture of root vegetables (including onions (clove-studded, if liked), leeks, carrots, turnip and swede) and put them in a large saucepan *(above left)*. Add mushroom stems, sliced celery, cabbage, parsley stalks and a bouquet garni. Pour in twice the depth of water or vegetable water *(above right)*, bring to the boil, then simmer for 1–2 hours. Strain, then season to taste.

CLARIFYING STOCK

For a jewel-like consommé, the stock must be clarified. Strain it into a clean non-aluminium pan. Whisk 2 egg whites to soft peaks; crush 2 eggshells. Add whites and shells to the soup and heat slowly, whisking until a thick white crust forms. Stop whisking, let the mixture foam up, then turn the heat off so that it falls in the pan. Repeat twice, then gently strain through a muslin-lined sieve.

DEGREASING

If time permits, chill the stock or soup: the fat will set to a solid round on top and can easily be lifted off. Alternatively, blot the surface with kitchen paper.

THICKENING SOUPS

Thicken cream soups with a butter and flour paste *(beurre manié)*. For every 250ml/8fl oz/ 1 cup of soup, use 15ml/1 tbsp each of plain flour and softened butter. Add small amounts of *beurre manié* at a time, stirring the soup well between additions.

The easiest way to thicken a vegetable soup, without adding extra fat or starch, is to scoop out some of the vegetables, purée them in a blender or food processor, then stir them back into the soup.

Oats make a very good thickener. You will need about 15ml/1 tbsp for every 600ml/ 1 pint/2½ cups of soup. Sprinkle over the soup about an hour before serving. Simmer, stirring occasionally.

11

Classic Soups

Cold Leek & Potato Soup

INGREDIENTS

450g / 1lb potatoes (about 3 large), peeled and cubed
1.5 litres / 2½ pints / 6¼ cups chicken stock
350g / 12oz (about 4) leeks
150ml / ¼ pint / ⅔ cup crème fraîche or soured cream, plus extra to garnish
salt and ground black pepper
45ml / 3 tbsp snipped fresh chives, to garnish

SERVES 6–8

1 Put the potatoes and stock in a saucepan or flameproof casserole and bring to the boil. Reduce the heat and simmer for 15–20 minutes.

2 Trim the leeks and make a slit along the length of each one with a sharp vegetable knife. Rinse them well under cold running water and then slice thinly.

3 When the potatoes are barely tender, stir in the leeks. Season with salt and pepper and simmer for 10–15 minutes until the vegetables are soft. Stir occasionally. If the soup appears too thick, thin it down with a little more stock or water.

4 Purée the soup in a food processor, or blender. If you would prefer a very smooth soup, press it through a coarse sieve. Stir in the crème fraîche or cream, cool and then chill. To serve, ladle into chilled bowls and garnish with a swirl of cream and snipped chives.

Gazpacho

INGREDIENTS

½ green pepper, seeded and coarsely chopped
½ red pepper, seeded and coarsely chopped
225g/8oz cucumber, coarsely chopped
1 large tomato, coarsely chopped
2 spring onions, chopped
Tabasco sauce (optional)
45ml/3 tbsp chopped fresh parsley or coriander
croûtons, to serve
SOUP BASE
450g/1lb ripe tomatoes, peeled, seeded,
and chopped
15ml/1 tbsp tomato ketchup
30ml/2 tbsp tomato purée
1.5ml/¼ tsp sugar
3.75ml/¾ tsp salt
5ml/1 tsp ground black pepper
50ml/2fl oz/¼ cup sherry vinegar
175ml/6fl oz/¾ cup olive oil
350ml/12fl oz/1½ cups tomato juice

SERVES 4

1 To make the soup base, put all the prepared tomatoes in a food processor or blender; pulse on and off until just smooth, scraping the sides of the container occasionally.

2 Add the ketchup, tomato purée, sugar, salt and pepper, sherry vinegar and oil. Pulse on and off 3–4 times, just to blend. Transfer to a large bowl. Stir in the tomato juice.

3 Put the peppers and the cucumber in the bowl of the food processor or blender and pulse on and off until they are finely chopped. Be careful not to overmix.

4 Reserve about 30ml/2 tbsp of the chopped vegetables for the garnish and then stir the remainder into the soup base. Check seasoning, then mix in the chopped tomato, spring onions, and a dash of Tabasco sauce, if liked. Chill well.

5 To serve, ladle the chilled soup into four bowls. Sprinkle each portion with the reserved chopped vegetables, chopped fresh parsley or coriander and a few croûtons.

Bouillabaisse

INGREDIENTS

*1.5kg/3lb white fish such as monkfish, John
Dory, red mullet, whiting or bass
900g/2lb oily fish such as mackerel or eel
2 large crabs
8 lobster tails
175ml/6fl oz/¾ cup olive oil
2 onions, sliced
2 leeks, trimmed and sliced
2 celery sticks, sliced
450g/1lb tomatoes, peeled, seeded and chopped
3 garlic cloves, crushed
bouquet garni
thinly peeled strip of orange rind
2 fresh fennel sprigs
1.2 litres/2 pints/5 cups fish stock
pinch of saffron strands steeped in 30ml/2 tbsp
boiling water
15ml/1 tbsp tomato purée
15ml/1 tbsp Pernod
salt and ground black pepper
45ml/3 tbsp chopped fresh parsley, to garnish*
MARINADE
*45ml/3 tbsp olive oil
2 garlic cloves, finely chopped
pinch of saffron in 30ml/2 tbsp
boiling water
chopped fresh parsley, to garnish*

SERVES 6

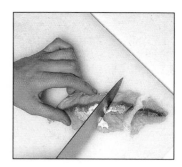

1 Discard the fins, then scale, skin and clean both the white and the oily fish. Cut the fish into chunks. Use the fish heads and tails to make the fish stock.

2 Make the marinade. Mix together the olive oil, garlic and saffron in a bowl. Pour this over the fish

3 Leave all the shellfish in their shells. Using a cleaver, chop the crab into pieces.

4 In a large flameproof casserole, heat the oil and sauté the onions, leeks and celery until soft. Add the tomatoes, garlic, bouquet garni, orange rind and fennel. Stir in the fish stock, the saffron with its liquid and season to taste. Bring to the boil and cook for 30–40 minutes. Twenty minutes before serving, add the oily fish and shellfish and boil hard, uncovered for 7 minutes. Put the white fish on top and boil for 5 minutes more. Discard the bouquet garni, orange rind and fennel sprigs.

5 Whisk the tomato purée and Pernod together and swirl it into the broth. Season well, to taste. Serve the bouillabaisse in heated bowls, garnished with chopped fresh parsley.

Mulligatawny Soup

INGREDIENTS

50g/2oz/¼ cup butter or 60ml/4 tbsp oil
2 large chicken joints, about 350g/12oz each
1 onion
1 carrot
1 small turnip
about 15ml/1 tbsp curry powder, to taste
4 cloves
6 black peppercorns, lightly crushed
50g/2oz/⅓ cup lentils
900ml/1½ pints/3¾ cups chicken stock
40g/1½oz/¼ cup sultanas
salt and ground black pepper

SERVES 4

1 Melt the butter or heat the oil in a large saucepan, then brown the chicken over a brisk heat. Transfer the chicken to a plate. Chop the onion, carrot and turnip with a sharp vegetable knife.

2 Add the chopped vegetables to the saucepan and then cook until lightly coloured. Stir in the curry powder, cloves and peppercorns and cook for 1–2 minutes.

3 Add the lentils to the pan and pour in the stock. Bring to the boil, then add the sultanas and chicken and any juices from the plate. Cover the pan and simmer the soup gently for about 1¼ hours.

4 Take the chicken from the pan and discard the skin and bones. Chop the flesh, return to the soup and reheat. Check the seasoning before serving the soup.

Borscht

INGREDIENTS

1 large cooking apple, chopped
1 onion, chopped
450g/1lb raw beetroot, peeled and chopped
2 celery sticks, chopped
½ red pepper, chopped
115g/4oz/1½ cups mushrooms, chopped
25g/1oz/2 tbsp butter
30ml/2 tbsp sunflower oil
2 litres/3½ pints/8 cups stock or water
5ml/1 tsp cumin seeds
pinch of dried thyme
1 large bay leaf
squeeze of fresh lemon juice
salt and ground black pepper
150ml/¼ pint/⅔ cup soured cream
fresh dill sprigs, to garnish

SERVES 6

19

2 Stir in the cumin seeds and cook for 1 minute, then add the remaining stock or water, dried thyme, bay leaf, lemon juice and seasoning. Bring to the boil, then cover and turn down to a gentle simmer. Cook for about 30 minutes.

3 Strain the vegetables and reserve the liquid. Purée the vegetables in a food processor or blender until they are smooth and creamy. Return the vegetables to the pan, stir in the reserved liquid and reheat. Check the seasoning.

1 Put the fruit and vegetables into a large pan with the butter, oil and 45ml/3 tbsp of the stock or water. Cover and cook gently for about 15 minutes.

4 Serve the borscht with swirls of soured cream, garnished with a few sprigs of fresh dill.

Minestrone with Pesto Toasts

INGREDIENTS

30ml / 2 tbsp olive oil
2 garlic cloves, crushed
1 onion, halved and sliced
225g / 8oz / 1½ cups diced lean bacon
2 small courgettes, quartered and sliced
50g / 2oz / ½ cup French beans, chopped
2 small carrots, diced
2 celery sticks, finely chopped
bouquet garni
50g / 2oz / ½ cup short cut macaroni
50g / 2oz / ½ cup frozen peas
½ x 425g / 15oz can red kidney beans,
drained and rinsed
50g / 2oz / ½ cup shredded green cabbage
4 tomatoes, peeled and seeded
salt and ground black pepper
TOASTS
8 slices of French bread
15ml / 1 tbsp ready-made pesto sauce
15ml / 1 tbsp grated Parmesan cheese

SERVES 4

1 Heat the olive oil in a large saucepan and gently fry the garlic and onion for 5 minutes, until just softened. Add the diced bacon, courgettes, French beans, carrots and celery to the pan and stir-fry for a further 3 minutes.

2 Pour about 1.2 litres/2 pints/5 cups cold water over the vegetables in the pan and add the bouquet garni. Cover the pan and simmer the soup for 25 minutes.

3 Add the macaroni, peas and kidney beans and cook for 8 minutes. Then add the cabbage and tomatoes and cook for 5 minutes more.

4 Meanwhile, make the toasts. Spread the bread slices with the pesto sauce, sprinkle a little Parmesan over each and brown lightly under a hot grill.

5 Remove the bouquet garni from the soup, season, and serve with the pesto toasts.

COOK'S TIP
If you are making this soup for children, you could replace the macaroni with coloured pasta shapes, such as shells, twists or bows.

20

French Onion Soup

INGREDIENTS

15g/ ½oz/ 1 tbsp butter
30ml/ 2 tbsp olive oil
4 large onions, thinly sliced
2-4 garlic cloves, finely chopped
5ml/ 1 tsp sugar
2.5ml/ ½ tsp dried thyme
30ml/ 2 tbsp plain flour
120ml/ 4fl oz/ ½ cup dry white wine
2 litres/ 3½ pints/ 8 cups chicken or beef stock
30ml/ 2 tbsp brandy (optional)
6-8 thick slices of French bread
1 garlic clove, peeled
350g/ 12oz Gruyère or Emmental cheese, grated

SERVES 6–8

I In a flameproof casserole or large saucepan, heat the butter and oil. Add the onions. Cook for 10–12 minutes until they are softened and turning brown. Add the garlic, sugar and thyme. Continue cooking over a medium heat for 30–35 minutes, until the onions are well browned, stirring frequently.

2 Sprinkle all the flour over the top and stir it in until thoroughly blended. Then stir in the white wine and chicken or beef stock and bring the liquid to the boil. Skim off any foam that rises to the surface, then reduce the heat and simmer gently for about 45 minutes. Stir in the brandy, if using.

3 Preheat the grill and carefully toast the French bread on both sides. Rub each slice of the toast with the garlic clove. Place six or eight oven-proof soup bowls on to a baking sheet and fill each one about three-quarters full with the onion soup from the casserole or saucepan.

4 Float one or two pieces of toast in each bowl. Top with the grated cheese, dividing it evenly, and grill about 15cm/6in from the heat for about 3–4 minutes, until the cheese begins to bubble. Serve the onion soup immediately, with its topping.

Fish & Meat Soups

Salmon Chowder

INGREDIENTS

20g / ¾oz / 1½ tbsp butter or margarine
1 onion, finely chopped
1 leek, finely chopped
65g / 2½oz / ½ cup finely chopped bulb fennel
25g / 1oz / ¼ cup plain flour
1.5 litres / 2½ pints / 6¼ cups fish stock
2 potatoes, cut in 1cm / ½in cubes
450g / 1lb boneless, skinless salmon, cut in
2cm / ¾in cubes
175ml / 6fl oz / ¾ cup milk
120ml / 4fl oz / ½ cup whipping cream
30ml / 2 tbsp chopped fresh dill
salt and ground black pepper

SERVES 4

1 Melt the butter or margarine in a large saucepan. Add the onion, leek and fennel and cook over a medium heat for about 5–8 minutes, until soft, stirring the mixture occasionally. Sprinkle the flour over the vegetables and stir in. Reduce the heat to low and cook, stirring occasionally with a wooden spoon, for 3 minutes.

2 Add the fish stock and potatoes and season with salt and pepper. Bring to the boil, then reduce the heat, cover, and simmer until all the potatoes are tender – this will take about 20 minutes.

3 Add the salmon pieces and simmer for about 3–5 minutes, until they are just cooked.

4 Stir in the milk, whipping cream and dill and cook until just warmed through; do not boil. Taste and add some more salt and pepper, if needed, then serve.

Saffron Mussel Soup

INGREDIENTS

40g / 1½oz / 3 tbsp unsalted butter
8 shallots, finely chopped
1 bouquet garni
5ml / 1 tsp black peppercorns
350ml / 12fl oz / 1½ cups dry white wine
1kg / 2¼lb mussels, scrubbed and debearded
2 leeks, trimmed and finely chopped
1 fennel bulb, finely chopped
1 carrot, finely chopped
several saffron strands steeped in 30ml / 2 tbsp
boiling water
1 litre / 1¾ pints / 4 cups fish or chicken stock
30-45ml / 2-3 tbsp cornflour, blended with
45ml / 3 tbsp cold water
120ml / 4fl oz / ½ cup whipping cream
1 tomato, peeled, seeded and finely chopped
30ml / 2 tbsp Pernod (optional)
salt and ground black pepper
chopped fresh dill, to garnish

SERVES 4–6

1 In a large saucepan, melt half the butter over a medium-high heat. Add half the shallots; cook for 1–2 minutes until softened but not coloured. Add the bouquet garni, peppercorns and white wine and bring to the boil. Add the mussels, cover tightly and cook over a high heat for 3–5 minutes, shaking the pan occasionally, until the mussels have opened.

2 Transfer the mussels to a bowl, then strain the cooking liquid through a muslin-lined sieve.

3 As the mussel shells cool down, pull them open and remove the mussels. Add any extra juices to the reserved liquid. Discard any closed mussels.

4 Rinse the pan and melt the remaining butter. Add the remaining shallots and cook for 1–2 minutes. Add the leeks, fennel, carrot and saffron and cook for 3–5 minutes, until softened.

5 Stir in the reserved cooking liquid, bring to the boil and cook for 5 minutes until the vegetables are tender and the liquid is slightly reduced. Add the stock and bring to the boil, skimming off any foam that rises to the surface. Season well and cook for a further 5 minutes.

6 Stir the blended cornflour into the soup. Simmer for 2–3 minutes until the soup thickens slightly, then stir in the cream, mussels and chopped tomato. Stir in the Pernod, if using, and cook for 1–2 minutes until hot. Check the seasoning and serve the soup at once, garnished with dill.

Fish Soup

INGREDIENTS

*1kg/2¼lb mixed fish or fish pieces (such as
coley, dogfish, whiting, red mullet or cod)
90ml/6 tbsp olive oil, plus extra to serve
1 onion, finely chopped
1 celery stick, chopped
1 carrot, chopped
60ml/4 tbsp chopped fresh parsley
175ml/6fl oz/¾ cup white wine
3 tomatoes, peeled and chopped
2 garlic cloves, finely chopped
1.5 litres/2½ pints/6¼ cups boiling water
salt and ground black pepper
rounds of French bread, to serve*

SERVES 6

1 Scale and clean the fish. Cut it into large pieces
and rinse well in cool water.

2 Heat the oil in a large saucepan and add the
onion. Cook over a low to moderate heat until it
begins to soften. Stir in the celery and carrot, and
cook for 5 minutes more. Add the parsley.

3 Pour over the
wine, raise the
heat, and cook
until reduced by
half. Stir in the
tomatoes and the
garlic then cook
for 3–4 minutes.
Stir occasionally.
Pour in the boiling water, and bring back to the
boil. Cook over a moderate heat for 15 minutes.

4 Stir in the fish, and simmer for 10–15 minutes,
or until tender. Season with salt and pepper.

5 Lift out the
cooked fish from
the saucepan with
a slotted spoon
and discard any
bones. Purée the
fish with the soup
in a blender or
food processor
until smooth. Taste for seasoning. If the soup is too
thick, add a little more water.

6 To serve, heat the soup to simmering. Toast the
rounds of French bread under the grill and sprinkle
them with olive oil. Place 2–3 rounds in each soup
plate before pouring over the hot soup.

New England Clam Chowder

INGREDIENTS

12 fresh clams, scrubbed
1.5 litres / 2½ pints / 6¼ cups water
40g / 1½ oz / ¼ cup finely diced salt pork
or streaky bacon
3 onions, finely chopped
1 bay leaf
5 potatoes, peeled and diced
475ml / 16fl oz / 2 cups milk, warmed
250ml / 8fl oz / 1 cup single cream
salt and ground black pepper
chopped fresh parsley, to garnish

SERVES 8

1 Rinse the clams well in cold water and drain. Place them in a deep fish kettle with the water and bring to the boil. Cover and steam for about 10 minutes, until the shells open. Remove from the heat.

2 When the clams have cooled slightly, remove them from their shells. Discard any clams that have not opened. Chop the clams roughly. Strain the cooking liquid through a sieve lined with muslin, and reserve it until required.

3 In a large heavy saucepan, fry the salt pork or bacon until it renders its fat and begins to brown. Add the onions and cook over a low heat for about 8–10 minutes, until softened.

4 Add the bay leaf, diced potatoes, and clam cooking liquid to the saucepan and stir well. Bring the soup to the boil and then cook for 5–10 minutes.

5 Stir in all the chopped clams and continue to cook until all the potatoes are tender, stirring occasionally. Add a little salt and pepper to taste.

6 Reduce the heat to low and stir in the warmed milk and cream. Simmer very gently for about 5 minutes more, then discard the bay leaf, and adjust the seasoning. Pour the soup into eight bowls and serve immediately, sprinkled with finely chopped fresh parsley.

Thai Chicken Soup

INGREDIENTS

15ml / 1 tbsp sunflower oil
1 garlic clove, finely chopped
2 large chicken breasts, skinned, boned and diced
2.5ml / ½ tsp ground turmeric
1.25ml / ¼ tsp hot chilli powder
75g / 3oz creamed coconut
1 litre / 1¾ pints / 4 cups hot chicken stock
30ml / 2 tbsp fresh lime or lemon juice
30ml / 2 tbsp crunchy peanut butter
50g / 2oz thread egg noodles, broken into short lengths
1 spring onion, finely chopped
15ml / 1 tbsp chopped fresh coriander
salt and ground black pepper
GARNISH
30ml / 2 tbsp desiccated coconut
½ red chilli, seeded and finely chopped

SERVES 4

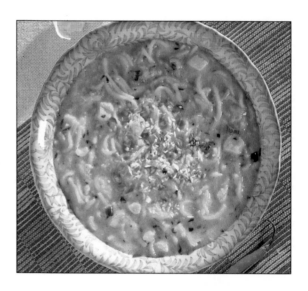

1 Heat the oil in a large saucepan. Fry the garlic until pale gold, then add the chicken and spices. Fry, stirring, for 3–4 minutes more.

2 Crumble the creamed coconut into the hot chicken stock in a jug; stir until dissolved, then add to the saucepan with the lime or lemon juice, peanut butter and egg noodles. Mix well.

3 Bring to the boil, stirring, then cover and simmer for 15 minutes. Add the spring onion, coriander, and plenty of salt and pepper. Cook for 5 minutes.

4 Meanwhile make the garnish by browning the coconut lightly with the chilli in a small ungreased frying pan. Stir the mixture constantly. Serve the soup in heated bowls, sprinkled with the browned coconut garnish.

Beef Chilli Soup

INGREDIENTS

15ml/1 tbsp oil
1 onion, chopped
175g/6oz/³⁄₄ cup minced beef
2 garlic cloves, chopped
1 red chilli, sliced
30ml/2 tbsp plain flour
400g/14oz can chopped tomatoes
600ml/1 pint/2¹⁄₂ cups beef stock
¹⁄₂ x 425g/15 oz can kidney beans, drained
salt and ground black pepper
30ml/2 tbsp chopped fresh parsley, plus extra
to garnish
crusty bread, to serve

SERVES 4

33

1 Heat the oil in a large pan. Fry the onion and minced beef for 5 minutes, stirring frequently to break up the meat, or until browned.

2 Add the garlic cloves, red chilli and flour to the pan and cook for 1 minute. Then add the tomatoes and pour in the stock. Bring the soup to the boil.

3 Stir in the drained kidney beans and season with salt and pepper to taste. Cook the soup over a medium heat for a further 20 minutes.

4 Add the chopped fresh parsley to the pan and check the seasoning. Pour the soup into four individual bowls and garnish with parsley. Serve with crusty bread.

Oriental Duck Consommé

INGREDIENTS

1 duck carcass (raw or cooked), plus 2 legs or
any giblets, trimmed of as much fat as possible
1 large onion, unpeeled, with root end trimmed
2 carrots, cut into 5cm/2in pieces
1 parsnip, cut into 5cm/2in pieces
1 leek, cut into 5cm/2in pieces
2-4 garlic cloves, crushed
2.5cm/1in piece of fresh root ginger,
peeled and sliced
15ml/1 tbsp black peppercorns
4-6 thyme sprigs, or 5ml/1 tsp dried thyme
1 small bunch coriander (6-8 sprigs),
leaves and stems separated
GARNISH
1 small carrot
1 small leek, halved lengthways
4-6 shiitake mushrooms, thinly sliced
soy sauce
2 spring onions, thinly sliced
finely shredded Chinese leaves
ground black pepper

SERVES 4

1 Put the duck, onion, carrots, parsnip, leek and garlic in a large pan or flameproof casserole. Add the ginger, peppercorns, thyme, and coriander stems, cover with cold water and bring to the boil, skimming any foam that rises to the surface.

2 Reduce the heat and simmer for 1½–2 hours, then strain through a muslin-lined sieve, discarding the bones and vegetables. Cool the duck stock and chill thoroughly. Skim off any congealed fat and blot the surface carefully with kitchen paper.

3 Make the garnish. Cut the carrot and leek into 5cm/2in pieces. Thinly slice each piece lengthways, then stack and slice into thin julienne strips. Place in a large saucepan with the mushrooms.

4 Pour over the stock and add a few dashes of soy sauce and some pepper. Bring to the boil, skimming any foam that rises to the surface. Add ground pep-  per to taste, then stir in the spring onions and Chinese leaves. Ladle the consommé into warmed bowls and sprinkle with the coriander leaves.

Vegetable Soups

Cream of Mushroom Soup

INGREDIENTS

450g/1lb open cup mushrooms, sliced
115g/4oz shiitake mushrooms, sliced
45ml/3 tbsp sunflower oil
1 onion, chopped
1 celery stick, chopped
1.2 litres/2 pints/5 cups stock or water
30ml/2 tbsp soy sauce
50g/2oz/¼ cup long-grain rice
300ml/½ pint/1¼ cups milk
salt and ground black pepper
chopped fresh parsley and almond flakes,
to garnish

SERVES 4–6

1 Put all the open cup and shiitake mushrooms in a large saucepan with the oil, onion and celery. Heat until sizzling, then cover and simmer for about 10 minutes, shaking the pan occasionally.

2 Add the stock or water, soy sauce, rice and seasoning. Bring to the boil then cover and simmer gently for 20 minutes until the vegetables and rice are tender.

3 Strain the vegetables, reserving the stock, and purée until smooth in a food processor or blender. Return the purée and the reserved stock to the saucepan.

4 Stir in the milk, reheat until boiling and taste for seasoning. Serve the soup hot, sprinkled with a little chopped parsley and a few almond flakes.

Provençal Vegetable Soup

INGREDIENTS

275g/10oz/1½ cups fresh broad
beans, shelled
2.5ml/½ tsp dried herbes de Provence
2 garlic cloves, finely chopped
15ml/1 tbsp olive oil
1 onion, finely chopped
1 large leek, finely sliced
1 celery stick, finely sliced
2 carrots, finely diced
2 small potatoes, finely diced
115g/4oz/¾ cup French beans
1.2 litres/2 pints/5 cups water
2 small courgettes, finely chopped
3 tomatoes, peeled, seeded and finely chopped
115g/4oz/1 cup shelled garden peas
handful of spinach leaves, cut into thin ribbons
salt and ground black pepper
sprigs of fresh basil, to garnish
PISTOU
1-2 garlic cloves, finely chopped
15g/½oz/½ cup (packed) basil leaves
60ml/4 tbsp grated Parmesan cheese
60ml/4 tbsp extra-virgin olive oil

SERVES 6–8

1 Make the pistou. Put the garlic, basil and cheese in a food processor or blender and process until smooth. Add the olive oil and process.

2 Place the broad beans in a pan with the herbes de Provence and 1 garlic clove. Add water to cover by 2.5cm/1in. Bring to the boil, reduce the heat and simmer for about 10 minutes until tender.

3 Heat the oil in a pan or flameproof casserole. Add the onion and leek, and cook for 5 minutes, stirring occasionally, until the onion just softens. Add the  celery, carrots and the remaining garlic clove and cook, covered, for 10 minutes, stirring occasionally.

4 Add the potatoes, French beans and water, then season lightly. Bring to the boil, skimming any foam that rises to the surface, then reduce the heat, cover and simmer gently for 10 minutes.

5 Add the courgettes, tomatoes, peas and the reserved beans and their cooking liquid. Simmer for 25–30 minutes. Add the spinach and simmer for 5 minutes more. Season, and serve, with some pistou swirled into each bowl. Garnish with basil.

Spiced Indian Cauliflower Soup

INGREDIENTS

1 large potato, peeled and diced
1 small cauliflower, chopped
1 onion, chopped
15ml/1 tbsp sunflower oil
1 garlic clove, crushed
15 ml/1 tbsp grated fresh ginger
10ml/2 tsp ground turmeric
5ml/1 tsp cumin seeds
5ml/1 tsp black mustard seeds
10ml/2 tsp ground coriander
1 litre/1¾ pints/4 cups vegetable stock
300ml/½ pint/1¼ cups natural yogurt
salt and ground black pepper
fresh coriander or parsley, to garnish

SERVES 4–6

2 Add the garlic, ginger and spices. Stir well and cook for 2 minutes, stirring occasionally. Pour in the stock and season well. Bring to the boil, then cover and

simmer for about 20 minutes. Stir in the yogurt, and serve garnished with fresh coriander or parsley. Alternatively, for a cold soup, chill in the fridge and add the garnish just before serving.

1 Put the diced potato, cauliflower and onion into a large pan with the oil and 45ml/ 3 tbsp water. Heat until the water is hot and bubbling, then cover and turn the heat down. Continue cooking the mixture for about 10 minutes, stirring occasionally.

40

Italian Vegetable Soup

INGREDIENTS

900ml/1½ pints/3¾ cups vegetable stock
1 bay leaf
1 small carrot, cut into 5cm/2in long
julienne strips
1 baby leek, cut into 5cm/2in long
julienne strips
1 celery stick, cut into 5cm/2in long
julienne strips
50g/2oz/½ cup green cabbage, finely sliced
115g/4oz/1 cup cooked cannellini beans
25g/1oz/¼ cup soup pasta, such as tiny
shells, bows, stars or elbows
salt and ground black pepper
snipped fresh chives, to garnish

SERVES 4

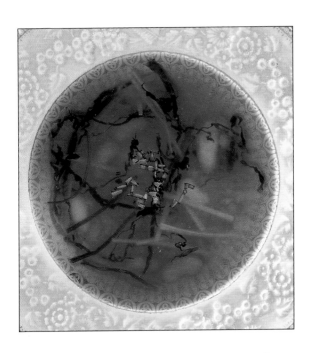

41

1 Put the stock and bay leaf into a large saucepan and bring to the boil. Add the carrot, leek and the celery, cover and simmer for 6 minutes. Add the cabbage, beans and pasta. Stir well, then simmer uncovered for about 4–5 minutes, or until all the vegetables and the pasta are tender.

2 Remove the bay leaf and season to taste. Ladle into four soup bowls and garnish with snipped chives. Serve the soup immediately.

COOK'S TIP
The success of this soup depends on the quality of the stock, so use home-made vegetable stock rather than stock cubes.

Leek, Parsnip & Ginger Soup

INGREDIENTS

30ml/2 tbsp olive oil
225g/8oz leeks, sliced
25g/1oz fresh root ginger, finely chopped
675g/1½lb parsnips, roughly chopped
300ml/½ pint/1¼ cups dry white wine
1.2 litres/2 pints/5 cups vegetable stock
or water
salt and ground black pepper
fromage frais and mild paprika, to garnish

SERVES 4–6

1 Heat the oil in a large saucepan and add the leeks and ginger. Cook gently for 2–3 minutes, until the leeks start to soften.

2 Add the chopped parsnips and cook gently for a further 7–8 minutes until softened.

3 Pour in the white wine and stock or water and bring to the boil. Reduce the heat and simmer for 20–30 minutes or until the parsnips are tender.

4 Purée the soup in a blender or food processor. Season to taste and reheat. Serve, garnished with a swirl of fromage frais and a dusting of paprika.

Broccoli & Almond Soup

INGREDIENTS

50g / 2oz / ½ cup ground almonds
675g / 1½lb broccoli
300ml / ½ pint / 1¼ cups skimmed milk
900ml / 1½ pints / 3¾ cups vegetable stock
salt and ground black pepper

SERVES 4–6

3 Place the rest of the almonds with the broccoli, milk and vegetable stock in a blender or food processor and blend well until smooth. Season the soup to taste.

4 Reheat the soup and serve immediately, sprinkled with the reserved toasted ground almonds.

43

I First, preheat the oven to 180°C/ 350°F/Gas 4 and spread the ground almonds evenly on a baking sheet. Toast them in the oven for about 10 minutes, or until golden brown. Reserve a quarter of the almonds and set aside for the garnish.

2 Cut the broccoli into small florets and steam for 6–7 minutes, or until tender. Check it frequently as the broccoli must be soft but not mushy.

New England Spiced Pumpkin Soup

INGREDIENTS

25g/1oz/2 tbsp butter
1 onion, finely chopped
1 small garlic clove, crushed
15ml/1 tbsp plain flour
pinch of grated nutmeg
2.5ml/½ tsp ground cinnamon
*350g/12oz/3 cups pumpkin, seeded, peeled
and cubed*
600ml/1 pint/2½ cups chicken stock
150ml/¼ pint/⅔ cup orange juice
5ml/1 tsp brown sugar
salt and ground black pepper
GARNISH
15ml/1 tbsp vegetable oil
*2 slices of Granary bread without crusts,
cut into cubes*
30ml/2 tbsp sunflower seeds

SERVES 4

1 Heat the butter in a large saucepan, add the onion and garlic and fry gently for 4–5 minutes, until softened. Stir in the flour, spices and pumpkin. Cover and cook gently for 6 minutes, stirring from time to time.

2 Pour in the chicken stock and the orange juice and add the brown sugar. Cover the saucepan with a lid and bring to the boil, then reduce the heat and simmer gently for about 20 minutes, or until all the pumpkin cubes have softened.

3 Pour half of the mixture into a blender or food processor and process until smooth. Return the soup to the pan with the remaining chunky mixture, stirring constantly. Season and heat through.

4 Now make the garnish. Heat the vegetable oil in a frying pan and fry the bread cubes gently until they just begin to turn brown. Add all the sunflower seeds and fry for 1–2 minutes. Drain the croûtons and sunflower seeds well on kitchen paper.

5 Serve the soup hot with some croûtons and seeds scattered over the top. Serve the rest separately.

44

Chilled Summer Soups

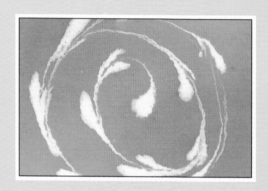

Watercress & Orange Soup

INGREDIENTS

1 large onion, chopped
15ml / 1 tbsp olive oil
2 bunches or bags of watercress
grated rind and juice of 1 large orange
600ml / 1 pint / 2½ cups vegetable stock
150ml / ¼ pint / ⅔ cup single cream
10ml / 2 tsp cornflour
salt and ground black pepper
a little thick cream or natural yogurt, to garnish
4 orange wedges, to serve

SERVES 4

1 Soften the onion in the oil in a pan. Trim off and discard any big stalks from the watercress and add it to the pan. Cover the pan and cook for about 5 minutes.

2 Add the orange rind and juice, and all the vegetable stock to the pan. Bring to the boil, lower the heat and cover. Simmer gently for about 10–15 minutes.

3 Put the soup in a blender or food processor and process thoroughly until smooth. Sieve the soup, if you like. Blend the cream with the cornflour and add it to the soup with seasoning to taste.

4 Bring the soup gently back to the boil, stirring until it is slightly thickened. Check the seasoning and then allow the soup to cool and chill it until required. Serve the soup with a swirl of thick cream or natural yogurt, and a wedge of orange to squeeze in at the last moment.

Green Pea & Mint Soup

INGREDIENTS

50g/2oz/4 tbsp butter
4 spring onions, chopped
450g/1lb peas, fresh or frozen
600ml/1 pint/2½ cups chicken or
vegetable stock
2 large mint sprigs
600ml/1 pint/2½ cups milk
pinch of sugar (optional)
salt and ground black pepper
single cream and small mint sprigs, to garnish

SERVES 4

1 Heat the butter in a large saucepan, add the spring onions, and cook gently until they are soft but not coloured, stirring occasionally.

2 Stir the peas into the pan, add the stock and mint and bring to the boil. Cover and simmer very gently for 30 minutes for fresh peas or 15 minutes if you are using frozen peas, until all the peas are very tender. Remove about 45ml/3 tbsp of the peas using a slotted spoon, and reserve for the garnish.

3 Pour the soup into a blender or food processor, add the milk and purée the soup until it is smooth. Season the soup to taste, adding a pinch of sugar, if you like. Allow the soup to cool, then cover and chill until you are ready to serve.

4 Pour the soup into bowls. Swirl a little cream into each, then garnish with mint and the reserved peas.

Chilled Fresh Tomato Soup

INGREDIENTS

1.5kg/3-3½lb ripe tomatoes, peeled and
roughly chopped
4 garlic cloves, crushed
30ml/2 tbsp extra-virgin olive oil (optional)
30ml/2 tbsp balsamic vinegar
ground black pepper
4 slices of wholemeal bread, to serve
fromage frais and chopped toasted hazelnuts,
to garnish

SERVES 4–6

1 Place all the chopped tomatoes in a blender or food processor with the garlic and olive oil, if using. Blend together well, scraping the sides, until smooth.

2 Pass the tomato and garlic mixture through a sieve to remove the seeds. Stir in the balsamic vinegar. Season to taste with pepper. Place the soup in the fridge to chill.

3 Toast the wholemeal bread lightly on both sides. While still hot, cut off the crusts and slice through horizontally to give two thin pieces. Gently rub off any doughy bits from the uncooked sides.

4 Cut each slice into four triangles. Place on a grill pan and toast the uncooked sides until pale golden. Watch constantly to prevent the toast from burning. Garnish each bowl of soup with a spoonful of fromage frais and a generous sprinkling of chopped hazelnuts. Serve with the Melba toast.

Chilled Asparagus Soup

INGREDIENTS

900g/2lb fresh asparagus
50g/2oz/4 tbsp butter or olive oil
175g/6oz/1½ cups sliced leeks or
spring onions
45ml/3 tbsp plain flour
1.5 litres/2½ pints/6¼ cups chicken stock
or water
120ml/4fl oz/½ cup single cream or
natural yogurt, plus extra to garnish
15ml/1 tbsp finely chopped fresh tarragon
or chervil
salt and ground black pepper

SERVES 6

3 Heat the butter or oil in a pan. Add the leeks or spring onions and cook until soft, then stir in the asparagus stalks, cover, and cook for 6–8 minutes.

4 Add the flour and stir well to blend. Cook for 3–4 minutes, uncovered, stirring occasionally.

5 Add the stock or water. Bring to the boil, stirring frequently, then reduce the heat and simmer for about 30 minutes. Season with salt and pepper.

1 Cut the top 6cm/2½in off the asparagus. Blanch these fine tips in boiling water for 5–6 minutes, until just tender. Drain. Cut each tip into 2–3 neat pieces.

6 Purée the soup in a blender or food processor. If necessary, strain it to remove any coarse fibres. Stir in the asparagus tips and the cream or yogurt, and the herbs. Cover the bowl and chill in the fridge. Stir thoroughly before serving, and check the seasoning. Garnish each portion with a swirl of cream or yogurt.

2 Trim the ends of the asparagus stalks, removing any brown or woody parts and chop the stalks into 1cm/½in pieces with a sharp kitchen knife.

Miami Chilled Avocado Soup

INGREDIENTS

2 large or 3 medium ripe avocados
15ml / 1 tbsp fresh lemon juice
75g / 3oz / ¾ cup roughly chopped, peeled cucumber
30ml / 2 tbsp dry sherry
20g / ¾oz / ¼ cup roughly chopped spring onions (with some of the green stems)
475ml / 16fl oz / 2 cups mild-flavoured chicken stock
5ml / 1 tsp salt
Tabasco sauce (optional)
natural yogurt or cream, to serve

SERVES 4

1 Halve, stone and peel the avocados. Chop the flesh and then process it in a blender or food processor, with the lemon juice, until you have a very smooth purée.

2 Add the cucumber, sherry and the spring onions. Process again until smooth.

3 In a large mixing bowl, combine the avocado mixture with the chicken stock using a hand whisk. Beat well until it is blended together. Season with the salt and a

few drops of the Tabasco sauce to taste, if liked. Cover the bowl with clear film and chill the soup for several hours.

4 To serve, fill four individual soup bowls with the avocado soup. Place a spoonful of natural yogurt or cream in the centre of each bowl and swirl carefully with a spoon to make a decorative pattern. Serve the chilled avocado soup immediately.

52

Melon & Basil Soup

INGREDIENTS

2 Charentais or cantaloupe melons
75g/3oz/⅓ cup caster sugar
175ml/6fl oz/¾ cup water
finely grated rind and juice of 1 lime
45ml/3 tbsp shredded fresh basil
fresh basil leaves, to garnish

SERVES 4–6

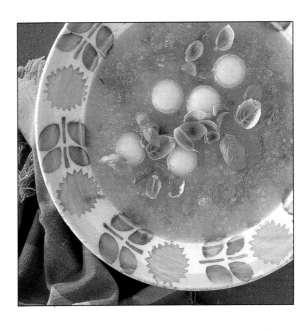

1 Cut the melons in half across the middle. Scrape out the seeds and discard. Using a melon baller, scoop out 20–24 balls and set aside for the garnish. Scoop out the remaining flesh and place it in a blender or food processor.

2 Place the sugar, water and lime rind in a small pan over a low heat. Stir until dissolved then bring to the boil and simmer for 2–3 minutes. Remove from the heat and cool slightly. Pour half the mixture into the blender or food processor with the scooped-out melon flesh. Blend until smooth, adding the remaining syrup and lime juice to taste.

3 Pour the soup into a bowl, stir in the basil and chill thoroughly. Serve garnished with basil leaves and the reserved melon balls.

COOK'S TIP
Take care to add the syrup in two stages, as the amount of sugar needed will depend on the sweetness of the melons you are using.

53

Bean, Lentil & Grain Soups

Smoked Turkey & Lentil Soup

INGREDIENTS

25g / 1oz / 2 tbsp butter
1 large carrot, chopped
1 onion, chopped
1 celery stick, chopped
1 leek, white part only, chopped
115g / 4oz / 1½ cups mushrooms, chopped
50ml / 2fl oz / ¼ cup dry white wine
1.2 litres / 2 pints / 5 cups chicken stock
10ml / 2 tsp dried thyme
1 bay leaf
115g / 4oz / ½ cup dried green lentils
225g / 8oz smoked turkey meat, diced
salt and ground black pepper
chopped fresh parsley, to garnish (optional)

SERVES 4

1 Melt the butter in a large saucepan. Add all the carrot, onion, celery, leek and mushrooms. Cook for about 3–5 minutes, until golden.

2 Stir in the wine and chicken stock. Bring to the boil and skim any foam that rises to the surface. Add the thyme and bay leaf. Lower the heat, cover, and simmer gently for 30 minutes.

3 Add the lentils, cover the saucepan and continue to cook the soup for 30–40 minutes more, until the lentils are tender. Stir the soup from time to time.

4 Stir in the diced turkey meat and season to taste with salt and pepper. Continue to cook the soup until just heated through. Ladle into four bowls and garnish with parsley, if you like.

Pasta & Bean Soup

INGREDIENTS

115g/4oz/scant ¾ cup dry beans (red kidney
and haricot beans), soaked in cold
water overnight
15ml/1 tbsp oil
1 onion, chopped
2 celery sticks, thinly sliced
2-3 garlic cloves, crushed
2 leeks, thinly sliced
1 vegetable stock cube
400g/14oz can or jar of pimientos, puréed
45-60ml/3-4 tbsp tomato purée
115g/4oz/1 cup pasta shapes
115g/4oz/1 cup baby sweetcorn, halved
50g/2oz/½ cup each broccoli and
cauliflower florets
a few drops of Tabasco sauce, to taste
salt and ground black pepper
PESTO BREAD
4 pieces of French bread
15ml/1 tbsp pesto sauce

SERVES 4

1 Drain the beans and place in a large pan with
1.2 litres/2 pints/5 cups water. Bring to the boil
for 10 minutes, then simmer for about 1 hour, or
until the beans are nearly tender.

2 When the beans are almost ready, heat the oil in a
large pan and fry the vegetables for 2 minutes. Add
the stock cube and the drained beans with about
600ml/1 pint/2½ cups of the liquid. Cover and
simmer for 10 minutes, stirring occasionally.

3 Add the puréed
pimientos to the
pan, stirring well,
then stir in the
tomato purée and
pasta. Cook for 15
minutes. Preheat
oven to 200°C/
400°F/Gas 6.

4 Make the pesto
bread. Spread the
French bread with
the pesto sauce.
Bake for 10 min-
utes in the pre-
heated oven until
they are starting to
turn crispy.

5 When the pasta is almost tender, add the sweetcorn, mixed broccoli and cauliflower florets,
Tabasco sauce and salt and pepper to taste. Heat
through for 2–3 minutes and serve at once with the
baked pesto-topped bread.

Split Pea Soup

INGREDIENTS

25g/1oz/2 tbsp butter
1 large onion, chopped
1 large celery stick with leaves, chopped
2 carrots, chopped
1 smoked gammon knuckle, about 450g/1lb
2 litres/3½ pints/8 cups water
350g/12oz/1½ cups split peas
30ml/2 tbsp chopped fresh parsley,
plus extra to garnish
2.5ml/½ tsp dried thyme
1 bay leaf
about 30ml/2 tbsp lemon juice
salt and ground black pepper

SERVES 4–6

1 Melt the butter in a large heavy-based saucepan. Add the onion, celery and carrots and cook until soft, stirring occasionally.

2 Add the remaining ingredients. Bring to the boil, cover and simmer gently for 2 hours, or until the split peas are very tender.

3 Lift out the gammon knuckle. Leave it to cool slightly, and then discard the skin and cut the meat from the bones. Cut the meat into small chunks.

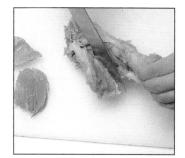

4 Return all the chunks of gammon to the saucepan. Discard the bay leaf. Taste the soup and add more lemon juice, salt and pepper, if required.

5 To serve, pour the hot soup into individual warmed soup bowls and garnish each serving with plenty of chopped fresh parsley.

58

Chicken & Chickpea Broth

INGREDIENTS

1 roast chicken carcass
1 onion, quartered
2 celery sticks, finely chopped
1 garlic clove, crushed
a few parsley sprigs
2 bay leaves
225g/8oz can chopped tomatoes
200g/7oz can chickpeas
30–45ml/2–3 tbsp leftover vegetables,
chopped, or 1 large carrot, finely chopped
15ml/1 tbsp chopped fresh parsley
2 slices of toast
25g/1oz/¼ cup grated cheese
salt and ground black pepper

SERVES 4

1 Pick off any little bits of flesh from the carcass, especially from the underside where there is often some very tasty dark meat. Set the flesh aside.

2 Place the chicken carcass, broken in half, in a large saucepan with the onion, half the celery, the garlic, herbs and sufficient water to cover. Cover the pan with a lid, bring to the boil and simmer for about 30 minutes, or until you are left with about 300ml/½ pint/1¼ cups of liquid.

3 Strain the stock and return it to the pan. Add the chicken flesh, the remaining celery, the tomatoes, chickpeas (and their liquid), vegetables and parsley. Season with salt and pepper to taste and simmer for another 7–10 minutes until heated through.

4 Sprinkle the toast evenly with the cheese and grill until bubbling. Cut the toast into neat fingers or quarters and serve with, or floating on top of, the finished soup.

Pasta & Lentil Soup

INGREDIENTS

225g/8oz/1 cup dried green or brown lentils
90ml/6 tbsp olive oil
50g/2oz/⅓ cup diced ham or salt pork
1 onion, finely chopped
1 celery stick, finely chopped
1 carrot, finely chopped
2 litres/3½ pints/8 cups chicken stock or
water, or a combination of both
1 fresh sage leaf or 4ml/¾ tsp dried sage
1 fresh thyme sprig or 1.5ml/¼ tsp
dried thyme
175g/6oz/2½ cups ditalini or other
small soup pasta
salt and ground black pepper
fresh coriander or flat-leaf parsley, to garnish

SERVES 4–6

1 Carefully check the lentils and remove any small stones. Place the lentils in a bowl, cover with cold water, and soak for 2–3 hours. Rinse and drain.

2 Heat the oil in a large saucepan and sauté the ham or pork for about 2–3 minutes. Add the finely chopped onion, and cook gently, until soft but not coloured.

3 Add the chopped celery and carrot. Cook for about 5 minutes more, stirring the soup frequently. Add the lentils, and stir well to coat them in the fats.

4 Pour in the chicken stock or water and add the herbs. Bring the soup to the boil. Cover with a lid and simmer over a moderate heat for about 1 hour or until the lentils are tender. Add salt and ground black pepper to taste.

5 Stir in the soup pasta, and cook it until it is just tender. Allow the soup to stand for a few minutes before pouring into individual heated bowls and garnishing with fresh coriander or parsley.

60

Barley & Vegetable Soup

INGREDIENTS

225g/8oz/generous 1 cup pearl barley,
preferably organic
2 litres/3½ pints/8 cups meat stock or water,
or a combination of both
45ml/3 tbsp olive oil
2 carrots, finely chopped
1 large onion, finely chopped
2 celery sticks, finely chopped
1 leek, thinly sliced
1 large potato, finely chopped
115g/4oz/⅔ cup diced ham
1 bay leaf
45ml/3 tbsp chopped fresh parsley
1 small fresh rosemary sprig
salt and ground black pepper
freshly grated Parmesan cheese, to serve (optional)

SERVES 6–8

1 Pick over the barley, and discard any stones or other particles. Wash it in cold water. Drain, then soak the barley in cold water for at least 3 hours.

2 Drain again and place the barley in a large pan with the stock or water. Bring to the boil, lower the heat and simmer for 1 hour. Skim off any scum.

3 Stir in the oil, all the vegetables and the ham. Add the herbs. If necessary, add more water – the ingredients should be covered by at least 2.5cm/1in. Simmer for

about 1–1½ hours, or until both the vegetables and the barley are very tender.

4 Taste for seasoning, adding salt and pepper as necessary. Serve the soup hot with freshly grated Parmesan cheese, if you like.

Rice & Broad Bean Soup

INGREDIENTS

1kg/2¼lb broad beans in their pods, or
400g/14oz shelled frozen broad
beans, thawed
90ml/6 tbsp olive oil
1 onion, finely chopped
2 tomatoes, peeled and finely chopped
225g/8oz/1 cup risotto rice
25g/1oz/2 tbsp butter
1 litre/1¾ pints/4 cups boiling water
salt and ground black pepper
freshly grated Parmesan cheese, to serve (optional)

SERVES 4

1 Shell the broad beans if they are fresh. Bring a large saucepan of water to the boil, and blanch the beans, fresh or frozen, for 3–4 minutes, then rinse the broad beans thoroughly under cold running water, and pop off the skins between fnger and thumb.

2 Heat the oil in a large saucepan. Add the onion. Cook over a low to moderate heat until it softens. Stir in the beans, and cook them gently for about 5 minutes, stirring often to coat them with the oil. Season with salt and pepper. Add the tomatoes, and cook for 5 minutes more, stirring often.

3 Stir in the rice. After 1–2 minutes add the butter, and stir until it melts. Pour in the boiling water, a little at a time, until the whole amount has been added. Taste for seasoning. Continue cooking the soup until the rice is tender. Serve hot, with freshly grated Parmesan cheese, if you like.

63

Index

Asparagus soup, chilled, 50
Avocado soup, Miami chilled, 52

Barley & vegetable soup, 62
Beef chilli soup, 33
Borscht, 19
Bouillabaisse, 16
Broad beans: rice & broad bean
    soup, 63
Broccoli & almond soup, 43

Cauliflower soup, spiced
    Indian, 40
Chicken: chicken & chick-pea
    broth, 59
    mulligatawny soup, 18
    Thai chicken soup, 32
Chickpeas: chicken & chick-pea
    broth, 59
Chillies: beef chilli soup, 33
Clam chowder, New England, 30

Duck consommé, oriental, 34

Fish: bouillabaisse, 16
Fish soup, 28
French onion soup, 22

Garnishes, 9
Gazpacho, 14
Green pea & mint soup, 48

Italian vegetable soup, 41

Leeks: cold leek & potato soup, 13
    leek, parsnip & ginger soup, 42
Lentils: pasta & lentil soup, 60
    smoked turkey & lentil soup, 55

Melon & basil soup, 53
Miami chilled avocado soup, 52
Minestrone with pesto toasts, 20
Mulligatawny soup, 18
Mushrooms: cream of mushroom
    soup, 37
Mussel soup, saffron, 26

New England clam chowder, 30
New England spiced pumpkin
    soup, 44

Onion soup, French, 22
Oriental duck consommé, 34

Parsnips: leek, parsnip & ginger
    soup, 42

Pasta & bean soup, 56
Pasta & lentil soup, 60
Peas: green pea & mint soup, 48
Provençal vegetable soup, 38
Pumpkin soup, New England
    spiced, 44

Rice & broad bean soup, 63

Saffron mussel soup, 26
Salmon chowder, 25
Smoked turkey & lentil
    soup, 55
Spiced Indian cauliflower
    soup, 40
Split pea soup, 58
Stocks: chicken stock, 10
    clarifying stock, 11
    fish stock, 10
    meat stock, 10
    vegetable stock, 11

Tomatoes: chilled fresh tomato
    soup, 49
    gazpacho, 14
Turkey: smoked turkey &
    lentil soup, 55

Vegetable soups, 36–44

Watercress & orange soup, 47